SPORTS POSITIONS

LACROSSE: MIDFIELDER

by Christina Earley

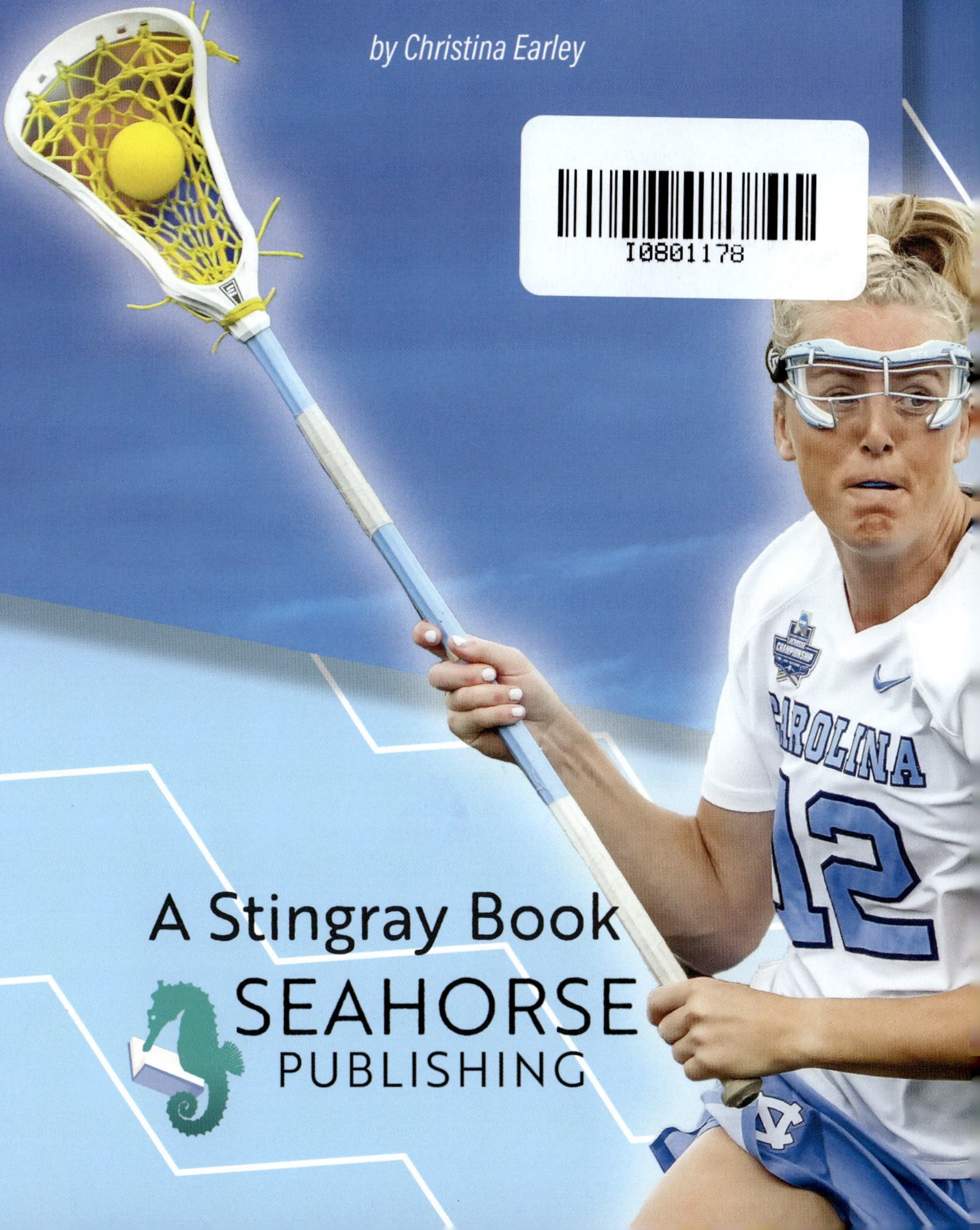

A Stingray Book

SEAHORSE PUBLISHING

Teaching Tips for Caregivers and Teachers:

This Hi-Lo book features high-interest subject matter that will appeal to all readers in intermediate and middle school grades. It may be enjoyed by students reading at or above grade level as well as by those who are looking for age-appropriate themes matched with a less challenging reading level. Hi-Lo books are ideal for ELL readers, too.

Each book appeals to a striving reader's age and maturity level. Opportunities are provided for students to read words they already know while encountering a limited number of new, high-interest vocabulary words. With these supports in place, students will read more fluently while increasing reading comprehension. Use the following suggestions to help students grow as readers.

- Encourage the student to read independently at home.
- Encourage the student to practice reading aloud.
- Encourage activities that require reading.
- Establish a regular reading time.
- Have the student write questions about what they read.

Teaching Tips for Teachers:

Before Reading

- Ask, "What do I know about this topic?"
- Ask, "What do I want to learn about this topic?"

During Reading

- Ask, "What is the author trying to teach me?"
- Ask, "How is this like something I already know?"

After Reading

- Discuss how the text features (headings, index, etc.) help with understanding the topic.
- Ask, "What interesting or fun fact did you learn?"

TABLE OF CONTENTS

WHAT IS A MIDFIELDER?

Midfielder is a position on a lacrosse team.

Midfielders play on both the **offensive** and **defensive** sides of the field.

They have one of the most important positions on the field. They are team leaders.

FUN FACT

The Tewaaraton Award honors the most outstanding college lacrosse player in America.

MARYLAND

helmet
shoulder pads
jersey
gloves
shorts
socks

UNIFORM

Lacrosse midfielders wear a jersey, shorts, and socks.

To protect their heads and faces, midfielders wear a helmet or goggles.

In men's lacrosse, midfielders also wear shoulder pads and gloves for protection. Gloves actually make it harder to grip the stick.

THE STICK

The most important piece of equipment for a lacrosse player is the stick.

The main parts are the head, shaft, and mesh.

The head is the top part of the stick. The shaft is the long part that the midfielder grips. The mesh is the net that holds the ball.

FUN FACT

NFL legend Jim Brown was a lacrosse midfielder in high school and college.

head
mesh
shaft

BEFORE THE GAME

Midfielders train to build **endurance** so they can easily cover the field.

They practice drills for playing **on-ball defense** and for picking up ground balls.

Eating well and staying hydrated provide fuel for the body.

On game day, midfielders stretch and work on stick skills.

DURING THE GAME

Midfielders play both offense and defense. Some specialize in one or the other. But they are required to play both.

Midfielders run and pass the ball up and down the length of the field. They are responsible for **transitions**. They chase loose balls and **clear** saved shots.

Of all the players on a lacrosse team, midfielders run the most.

FUN FACT

Lacrosse player Nick Diegel holds the record for the fastest shot at 127.4 miles (205 kilometers) per hour!

PRINCETON
15
BROW

HISTORY

Lacrosse is the oldest team sport in North America.

A version of the game was first played by Native American tribes. They played on land that is now the northeastern United States and southeastern Canada.

A dentist from Canada created standard rules in 1867.

The first women's lacrosse game was played in Scotland in 1890.

FUN FACT

Lacrosse games played by Native Americans could have hundreds of players on each team.

TRAITS OF A GREAT MIDFIELDER

Midfielders must be good at staying calm under pressure.

They need good **athleticism** to run up and down the field and create fast breaks.

Mental toughness and the ability to correct mistakes quickly are also important.

33

NOTES FROM THE COACH

- Be a leader on and off the field.
- Listen and take constructive criticism from coaches and teammates.
- Admit mistakes and improve.
- Have **grit** to never give up even when things are tough.
- Learn all parts of the game and all positions.
- Work hard during practices and in games.
- Eat a well-balanced diet.
- Have a good attitude and be respectful to others.

G.O.A.T. Greatest of All Time

CHERIE GREER BROWN

College: University of Virginia

- NCAA National Champion 1991, 1993
- Defensive Player of the Year 1994
- First-Team All-American 1992, 1993, 1994

TAYLOR CUMMINGS

College: University of Maryland

- Tewaaraton Award winner 2014, 2015, 2016
- World Champion 2017
- First-Team All-American 2013, 2014, 2015, 2016

KEVIN FINNERAN

College: Ohio Wesleyan University

- NLL Champion 1994, 1995, 1998, 2001, 2003
- First-Team All-League 1998
- 235 career goals

A.J. HAUGEN

College: Johns Hopkins University

- First-Team All-American 1998, 1999, 2000
- Six-time MLL All-Star
- MLL Champion 2001, 2003

KELLY AMONTE HILLER

College: University of Maryland

- First-Team All-American 1994, 1995, 1996
- NCAA National Champion 1995, 1996
- Defensive Player of the Year 1995

ROBERT SHEK

College: Towson University

- First-Team All-American 1991
- Midfielder of the Year 1991
- World Champion 1994, 1998

TIM SOUDAN

College: University of Massachusetts Amherst

- Second-Team All-American 1989, 1990
- World Champion 1994, 1998
- MLL Champion 1997

MARY MCCARTHY STEFANO

College: Pennsylvania State University

- NCAA National Champion 1987
- First-Team All-American 1985, 1986, 1987
- Beth Allen Award winner 1994

RYAN WADE

College: University of North Carolina

- NCAA National Champion 1991
- Midfielder of the Year 1993
- World Championship MVP 1998

SANDY BRYAN WEATHERALL

College: Dartmouth College

- First-Team All-American 1982, 1983
- World Champion 1982, 1989
- Dartmouth record for most points in a game (12)

GLOSSARY

athleticism (ath·LE·tuh·si·zuhm): athletic ability; having the speed, strength, and agility of an athlete

clear (kleer): to accept a ball that has been saved by the goalie and then quickly run or pass it to the opposite/offensive side of the field

defensive (di·FEN·siv): defending; related to the team that is trying to keep the other team from scoring

endurance (en·DOOR·uhns): the ability to do something difficult for a long time

grit (grit): courage and strength of character

offensive (uh·FEN·siv): attacking; related to the team that is trying to score

on-ball defense (awn-bawl di·FENS): the act of defending a player who is carrying the ball; trying to keep a player who has the ball away from the goal

transitions (tran·ZISH·uhnz): times when the ball moves quickly from one side of the field to the other or from defense to offense

INDEX

AFTER READING QUESTIONS

1. Why do lacrosse midfielders need endurance?
2. Who invented the game of lacrosse?
3. Explain how the midfielder helps the offense and the defense.

About the Author

Christina Earley lives in sunny Florida with her husband and son. She has always loved different sports. She enjoys traveling to see different stadiums, arenas, and ballparks where she always has to eat the local hot dog.

Written by: Christina Earley
Design by: Kathy Walsh
Editor: Kim Thompson

Library of Congress PCN Data
Lacrosse: Midfielder / Christina Earley
Sports Positions
ISBN 978-1-6389-7643-1 (hard cover)
ISBN 978-1-6389-7644-8 (paperback)
ISBN 978-1-6389-7645-5 (EPUB)
ISBN 978-1-6389-7646-2 (eBook)
Library of Congress Control Number: 2022942727

Printed in the United States of America.

Photographs/Shutterstock: Cover, p 3 ©Scott Serio/Cal Sport Media/Newscom, Paparacy, Express Vectors; p 3-22 Express Vestors; p 5, 6, 9, 10, 13, 14, 17, 18, Paparacy; p 5 Gregory Vasil/ Cal Sport Media/Newscom; p 6 JoeSAPhotos; p 9 Scott Serio/Cal Sport Media/Newscom; p 10 Westend61 / Ignacio Ferrándiz Roig; p 13 Erica Denhoff/Icon Sportswire/Newscom; p 14 Andy Mead/YCJ/Icon/Newscom Sportswire; p 16 Erica Denhoff/Icon Sportswire/Newscom; p 18 Erica Denhoff/Icon Sportswire/Newscom

Seahorse Publishing Company
www.seahorsepub.com

Published in the United States
Seahorse Publishing
PO Box 771325
Coral Springs, FL 33077

SEAHORSE PUBLISHING